EXPLORING THE
GREAT LAKES

VISITING
THE GREAT LAKES

Gareth Stevens
PUBLISHING

By Michael Rajczak

Please visit our website, www.garethstevens.com. For a free color catalog of all our high-quality books, call toll free 1-800-542-2595 or fax 1-877-542-2596.

Library of Congress Cataloging-in-Publication Data

Rajczak, Michael.
Visiting the Great Lakes / by Michael Rajczak.
p. cm. — (Exploring the Great Lakes)
Includes index.
ISBN 978-1-4824-1204-8 (pbk.)
ISBN 978-1-4824-1194-2 (6-pack)
ISBN 978-1-4824-1436-3 (library binding)
1. Great Lakes (North America) — Juvenile literature. I. Rajczak, Michael. II. Title.
F551.R35 2015
977—d23

First Edition

Published in 2015 by
Gareth Stevens Publishing
111 East 14th Street, Suite 349
New York, NY 10003

Copyright © 2015 Gareth Stevens Publishing

Designer: Michael J. Flynn
Editor: Kristen Rajczak

Photo credits: Cover, p. 1 Flashon Studio/Shutterstock.com; p. 5 Map Resources/ Shutterstock.com; p. 6 Pincasso/Shutterstock.com; p. 7 Carl Ballou/Shutterstock.com; p. 8 Le Do/Shutterstock.com; p. 9 Josef Hanus/Shutterstock.com; pp. 10–11 (Chicago) Songquan Deng/Shutterstock.com; p. 11 (map) courtesy of NASA; p. 13 Robert F. Sisson/ National Geographic/Getty Images; p. 15 (Marblehead Lighthouse) Doug Lemke/ Shutterstock.com; p. 15 (Split Rock Lighthouse) Geoffrey Kuchera/Shutterstock.com; p. 16 ehrlif/Shutterstock.com; p. 17 courtesy of NOAA; p. 18 Dan Thornberg/Shutterstock.com; p. 19 Matt Jeppson/Shutterstock.com; p. 20 Birdiegal/Shutterstock.com; p. 21 Horst Petzold/Shutterstock.com; p. 22 ValeStock/Shutterstock.com; p. 23 Raymond Boyd/Michael Ochs Archives/Getty Images; p. 25 Ed Reschke/Photolibrary/Getty Images; p. 27 PR Newswire/AP Images; pp. 28–29 Nikitsin.smugmug.com/Shutterstock.com.

Printed in the United States of America

CPSIA compliance information: Batch #CS15GS: For further information contact Gareth Stevens, New York, New York at 1-800-542-2595.

CONTENTS

Words in the glossary appear in **bold** type
the first time they are used in the text.

The Great Lakes are five freshwater lakes in North America, including Lakes Huron, Ontario, Michigan, Erie, and Superior. The Great Lakes **basin** contains about 20 percent of all the freshwater in the world.

These lakes make up part of the United States' northern border. About 10 percent of the US population live in the Great Lakes region. The southern Canadian border along the Great Lakes is entirely in the **province** of Ontario. More than 30 percent of Canadians live around the Great Lakes.

The Great Lakes region is **unique**. From big cities to beautiful beaches, it's a great place to visit!

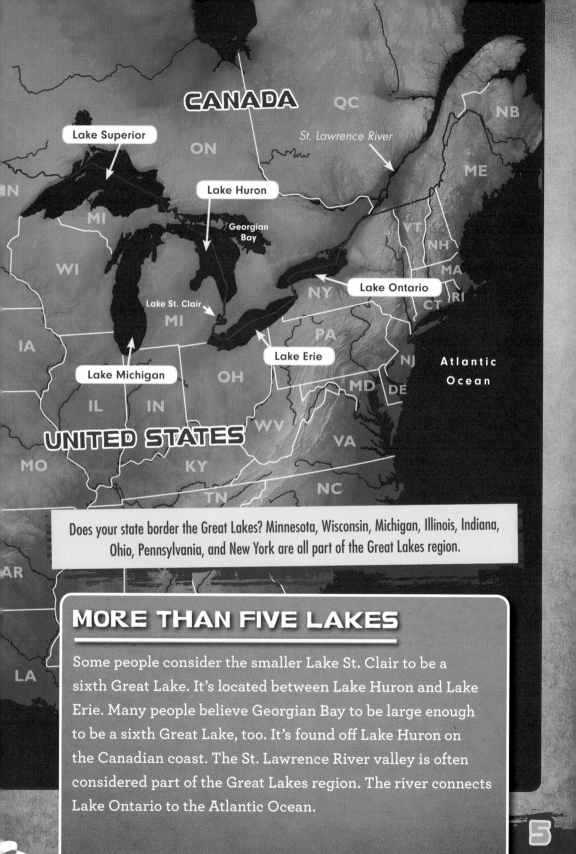

CANADA

QC

NB

Lake Superior

ON

St. Lawrence River

ME

Lake Huron

MI

Georgian Bay

VT

NH

MA

Lake Ontario

WI

NY

RI

Lake St. Clair

CT

MI

PA

IA

Lake Michigan

NJ

Atlantic Ocean

OH

MD

DE

IL

IN

UNITED STATES

WV

VA

MO

KY

NC

TN

Lake Erie

Does your state border the Great Lakes? Minnesota, Wisconsin, Michigan, Illinois, Indiana, Ohio, Pennsylvania, and New York are all part of the Great Lakes region.

MORE THAN FIVE LAKES

Some people consider the smaller Lake St. Clair to be a sixth Great Lake. It's located between Lake Huron and Lake Erie. Many people believe Georgian Bay to be large enough to be a sixth Great Lake, too. It's found off Lake Huron on the Canadian coast. The St. Lawrence River valley is often considered part of the Great Lakes region. The river connects Lake Ontario to the Atlantic Ocean.

ON THE BORDER

To fully enjoy all the Great Lakes region has to offer, you would need to cross the international border between Canada and the United States. Though policed by both nations, it's part of the longest peaceful border in the world.

Crossing from one country to the other requires proper identification such as a passport. This is true when traveling by boat on one of the lakes—even if you don't go ashore. Some of the most popular places to cross from one country to the other are between Niagara Falls, New York, and Niagara Falls, Ontario, and between Detroit, Michigan, and Windsor, Ontario.

A GREAT RESOURCE

The water of the Great Lakes is a resource shared by the United States and Canada. State governors and the premiers of Ontario and Québec have signed international agreements to protect the lakes and the St. Lawrence River. They've agreed to manage and protect this important resource together. This includes monitoring water usage, water quality, and water levels.

The Ambassador Bridge links Detroit and Windsor.

HOW DO THE GREAT LAKES CONNECT?

In the Great Lakes region, there are many more waterways than just the five main lakes. Some are natural, such as the St. Marys River that connects Lake Superior and Lake Huron. The Mackinac Strait connects Lakes Michigan and Huron, and Lake Huron connects to Lake Erie by way of the St. Clair River, Lake St. Clair, and the Detroit River.

Other waterways are man-made—and pretty cool to visit! The Soo **Locks** on the St. Marys River allow boats to bypass the river's roughest waters. The Welland Canal in Ontario was constructed in the 1950s to accommodate water elevation differences between Lakes Erie and Ontario.

Mackinac Strait

COOL CONNECTION FACTS

- Geologically, Lakes Michigan and Huron can be considered two parts of one bigger lake.

- The St. Lawrence Seaway project was completed in 1959. It made the final connections between bodies of water in the Great Lakes region and St. Lawrence River valley so that ships can travel this route to and from the Atlantic Ocean.

- The Mississippi River actually connects to Lake Michigan by the Illinois Waterway. This includes the Illinois River, Chicago River, and the Chicago Sanitary and Ship Canal.

The waterways throughout the Great Lakes region, such as the Welland Canal, make it possible to travel from one end of the basin to the other by boat. It takes about 9 days to cover the more than 2,000 miles (3,219 km) from the Atlantic Ocean to the port of Duluth-Superior in Minnesota.

CITIES OF THE GREAT LAKES

Two of the most populous cities in North America are found on the Great Lakes—Chicago, Illinois, and Toronto, Ontario. Many other big cities have developed on the Great Lakes, too. Most began as trading ports and became large **metropolitan** regions. The shipping of crops and natural resources along the Great Lakes caused the growth of some cities, and others, such as Detroit and Hamilton, Ontario, grew as centers of manufacturing.

ENJOY TORONTO

Spectacular Toronto is the largest city in Canada—and it's still growing! It's a truly international city with many business headquarters and world-class theater and arts. It's home to the Hockey Hall of Fame and several professional sport teams. Toronto has a lively waterfront, a huge science museum, and a wonderful zoo.

Milwaukee, Wisconsin; Toledo, Ohio; and Rochester, New York, are some of the large American cities on the Great Lakes. Mississauga and St. Catharines, Ontario, are two Canadian cities on Lake Ontario.

Home to around 2.7 million people, Chicago is the third-largest US city. About 9.5 million people live in the Chicago metropolitan area!

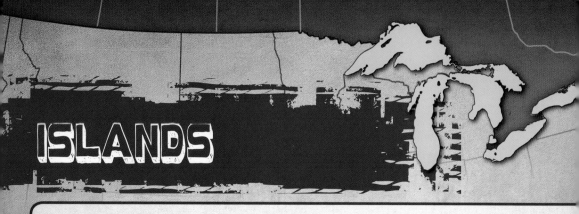

ISLANDS

Tourists have much more to look forward to in the Great Lakes region than just big cities! There are more than 35,000 islands in the Great Lakes basin. About half of that number are off Lake Huron in Georgian Bay. Thirteen others are grouped together in Toronto's harbor.

Some islands have residents who have built shoreline homes, such as the 20,000-person community on Grand Island in the Niagara River in New York. But many islands are only home to wildlife.

Mackinac Island in Lake Michigan is a theme park. When you step off the ferry, you're in a 19th-century village!

MANITOULIN ISLAND

Manitoulin Island, Ontario, is the largest island in the Great Lakes region—and the largest freshwater island in the world! It even contains a large freshwater lake of its own! On Manitoulin Island, visitors will find fantastic views, excellent fishing, and nature trails. The island is home to the Wikwemikong Indian Reserve, too. More than 3,000 members of the Wikwemikong live on the reserve.

There are about 1,500 islands included in the Thousand Islands in the St. Lawrence River.

LIGHTHOUSES AND SHIPWRECKS

Many of the attractions around the Great Lakes exist because of the unique features of the region. With so many islands and harbors, lighthouses were built all around the Great Lakes. In fact, there are about 325 of them! The oldest is the Marblehead Lighthouse at the entrance to Sandusky Bay in Ohio. It's been in continuous operation since it was built in 1822.

The Split Rock Lighthouse near Two Harbors, Minnesota, was built partly in response to storms in 1905 that sunk about 30 ships in Lake Superior. It's 54 feet (16.5 m) tall and sits atop a 130-foot (40 m) tall cliff.

WHAT'S THE PURPOSE OF LIGHTHOUSES?

Lighthouses look like towers. They're built on shorelines to help guide ships safely. Many are brightly colored to be visible during the day. Powerful lights that sweep back and forth or flash make their locations known at night and in foggy conditions. Lighthouses may mark places where rocks are present below the waterline. Others mark entrances of a harbor or channel.

Split Rock Lighthouse

Marblehead Lighthouse

The Great Lakes' lighthouses are interesting stops on a trip through the region. Some have visitors' centers with historical information and tours—you might be able to climb to the top of the light!

The Great Lakes are famous for rough storms. That's why as many as 2,000 shipwrecks are located beneath the surface of Lake Erie alone! Whitefish Point in Lake Superior is known as the "graveyard of ships" because so many have been lost there.

It's common for one or two lost ships to be located by researchers each year. In September 2013, a schooner called *Ocean Wave* was found in Lake Ontario. It sank in 1890! Would you like to see one of these shipwrecks? Some can be explored using diving gear and the help of a guide, such as those working with the Great Lakes Shipwreck Historical Society.

Sometimes shipwrecks wash ashore, like this one on the shore of Lake Superior.

THE WRECK OF THE EDMUND FITZGERALD

Twenty-nine men died November 10, 1975, aboard the *Edmund Fitzgerald* in Lake Superior. A bulk freighter, the *Edmund Fitzgerald* was carrying more than 26,000 tons (23,582 mt) of cargo. Its captain, Ernest McSorley, said over the radio that the ship was in the worst weather he had ever seen. Today, the ship lies in two parts in about 530 feet (162 m) of water.

This shipwreck rests at the bottom of Lake Huron.

FISHING

The Great Lakes themselves provide much of the most popular recreation in the region. Both commercial and sport fishing are common in the **watershed**. More than 170 kinds of fish live around the Great Lakes. In some places, you can drop in a line yourself from a dock or boat. There are also many boat tours with a crew who can put you right into fishing hot spots.

Lake Erie is a great place to fish for yellow perch and walleye. Lake St. Clair and the Niagara River are very popular with bass fishermen. Lake Ontario is famous for huge Pacific salmon and rainbow trout.

walleye

TIME TO EAT!

It's no surprise that many people around the Great Lakes eat the fish they catch! When a fisherman has caught a large enough fish, the scales and bones need to be cut away. This leaves the fleshy fillets that are good to eat. Would you want to fry your fish with butter and spices or lemon? How about coated with breadcrumbs or batter?

There are fishing laws on all the Great Lakes. Some were put in place to stop overfishing of some kinds of fish.

BIRDING

There are almost 11,000 miles (17,700 km) of shoreline in the Great Lakes region that are home to many kinds of birds. Lake Erie has been called the most bird-rich **ecosystem** in the United States. An amazing number and variety of **migrating** birds navigate over and around Lake Erie.

Many eagles are year-round residents of the Great Lakes, though some migrate, too. Ospreys and northern harriers can be found during the summer months. Canada geese, common loons, and trumpeter swans migrate through the Great Lakes each year, too. Even more numerous are the varieties of ducks and seagulls that call the Great Lakes region home.

northern harrier

LAKE ERIE BIRDING TRAIL

Along the length of the shore of Lake Erie in Ohio, there's a 312-mile (502 km) trail for dedicated bird-watchers. The Lake Erie Birding Trail stretches from Conneaut to Toledo, Ohio, and offers views of hundreds of kinds of birds, including waterfowl and songbirds. There are even birding events along the trail organized by local bird-watching organizations.

Many different species of birds inhabit the Great Lakes region.

ALL ASHORE!

Another way to enjoy the Great Lakes is by boat! Boating is a common pastime of Great Lakes residents and visitors alike. Whether you spend the day on a rented fishing boat or take a dinner cruise around a city, views from the water offer a unique look at the region.

You can take a 12-day cruise on the St. Lawrence River from Montreal, Québec, to Chicago, visiting Kingston, Ontario, and the Welland Canal along the way. An 11-day cruise from Buffalo takes you through Lake Erie, the Detroit River, and Lake St. Clair on the way to Duluth, Minnesota.

MARINAS

Marinas are found all around the Great Lakes. A marina is like a parking lot for boats. Many have docks you can rent for a few days or a whole season. Marinas often offer help with needed repairs and other boat services, like fuel or cleaning. At the end of the boating season, many marinas offer winter storage for boats.

Many cities and towns around the Great Lakes have sunset and moonlight cruises for a few hours. One is aboard the *Detroit Princess* Riverboat!

BEACHES

Summer is an excellent time to take advantage of the many beaches along the Great Lakes. Lake Superior Provincial Park in Ontario covers about 618 square miles (1,600 sq km) on the eastern coast of Lake Superior and has several beaches. Neys Provincial Park on the western shore of Lake Superior is so beautiful, it's been painted by several artists.

On Lake Erie, the Headlands Beach State Park includes the largest natural beach in Ohio. Presque Isle State Park in Erie, Pennsylvania, is a sandy **peninsula** featuring 11 beaches.

Many of the beaches in state parks have winter activities, too! Cross-country skiing and snowshoeing groups enjoy nature even in the cold.

SAND DUNES IN MICHIGAN?

Michigan has more than 300,000 acres (121,500 ha) of sand **dunes**! So, if there's a place for beach lovers in the Great Lakes region, it might be around Lake Michigan. The Silver Lake Sand Dunes found between Lake Michigan and Silver Lake draw about 1 million people every year. The huge mountains of sand are just one example of the unique dunes you can visit in Michigan.

Climbing Sleeping Bear Dunes on Lake Michigan can be fun—but it's tiring!

Here are a few more places you might enjoy on a trip around the Great Lakes!

Cedar Point, Sandusky, Ohio
This popular amusement park features award-winning roller coasters, a water park, and a beach.

Boldt Castle, Thousand Islands
Visit a **genuine** castle that was built in the early 1900s by a wealthy hotel owner in the beautiful Thousand Islands in the St. Lawrence River.

Sauble Beach, Ontario
Sauble Beach is the second-largest freshwater beach in the world at about 7 miles (11 km) long.

Grand Haven State Park, Michigan
The shores of Lake Michigan have something for every lover of the outdoors including camping, boating, fishing, and the Grand Haven Pier and Lighthouse.

ONTARIO'S NIAGARA FALLS

Niagara Falls, Ontario, and the surrounding region along the Niagara River may be the ultimate tourist destination. Hotels tower over the legendary waterfalls. Wax museums and amusements line popular Clifton Hill. The scenic Niagara Parkway winds along the river and **gorge**, leading to historic Fort Erie and Fort George. There are even fireworks over the falls every week!

Would you be scared or excited to ride the huge roller coasters at Cedar Point?

HOW'S THE WEATHER?

Now that you know all about what you can do when visiting the Great Lakes, what should you pack? That depends on what time of year you go. The Great Lakes region experiences all four seasons. The southern areas along Lake Erie and lower Lake Michigan tend to be warmer than the northern shores along Lake Superior and Lake Huron in Canada.

However, the lakes can change the weather of the region no matter the season. In the summer, the lakes provide a cooling effect. In the winter, icy winds out of Canada passing over the lakes can cause big lake-effect snowstorms.

LAKE EFFECT WEATHER

The weather in the Great Lakes can be influenced by many factors, but the greatest of these is the lakes themselves. The temperature difference between the lakes and the surrounding land causes light winds called land breezes and lake breezes. Sometimes the temperature differences between the lakes and the air mass passing over them can cause thunderstorms.

Keep in mind the season when visiting the Great Lakes. It can be hot in the summer and below freezing in the winter!

basin: an area that drains water from surrounding land

dune: a sand hill created by wind

ecosystem: all the living things in an area

genuine: true, real

gorge: a narrow, steep-walled canyon or part of a canyon

lock: a closed area in a canal used to raise or lower boats as they pass from one water level to another

metropolitan: having to do with a city and its surrounding suburbs and towns

migrating: moving from one place to another, sometimes because of changing seasons

peninsula: an area of land nearly surrounded by water and connected to a main body of land

province: a political unit of a country

tourist: someone who travels to visit a place

unique: being the only one of its kind

watershed: an area of land whose water drains into a particular river or waterway

BOOKS

Marsh, Carole. *The Mystery on the Great Lakes.* Peachtree City, GA: Gallopade International, 2009.

Piehl, Janet. *The Great Lakes.* Minneapolis, MN: Lerner Publishing, 2010.

WEBSITES

All Great Lakes Lighthouses
gllka.com/resources/lighthouses/index.htm
This website links to every lighthouse on the Great Lakes.

Great Facts About the Five Great Lakes
www.livescience.com/29312-great-lakes.html
Read many interesting facts about the Great Lakes on this website.

Great Lakes Facts and Figures
www.great-lakes.net/lakes/ref/lakefact.html
The Great Lakes Information Network provides lots of information about the lakes.

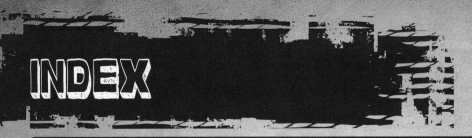

INDEX